INTRODUCTION

"Something New" introduces and expla_____ ration cake with a finished look of broderie a____ soft roll-over icing and royal icing are used. I_____ derie anglaise needs to stand away from the e_____ sides of the cake with royal icing, the end re_____ is very successful.

The variations on a theme are endless and the objectives of this book are to show the keen cake-decorator the new idea and enable people to develop their skills and imagination.

EQUIPMENT LIST

- Broderie Anglaise cutters
- Ribbon threading tool
- Straight Garrett frill
- Small aspic cutters
- Greaseproof paper
- Paintbrush
- Rolling pin
- Mixing machine for royal icing or bowl and wooden spoon

- Palette knife
- Cocktail sticks
- Ribbon
- Matchsticks
- Turntable
- Food colouring
- Piping tubes: 1, 0, 00
- Straight plastic scraper
- Scissors

For the cake you will need:

- Cake board
- Egg white
- Icing sugar

- Apricot jam
- Marzipan
- Sugar paste

BRODERIE ANGLAISE CUTTERS
(BABER FRILL CUTTERS)

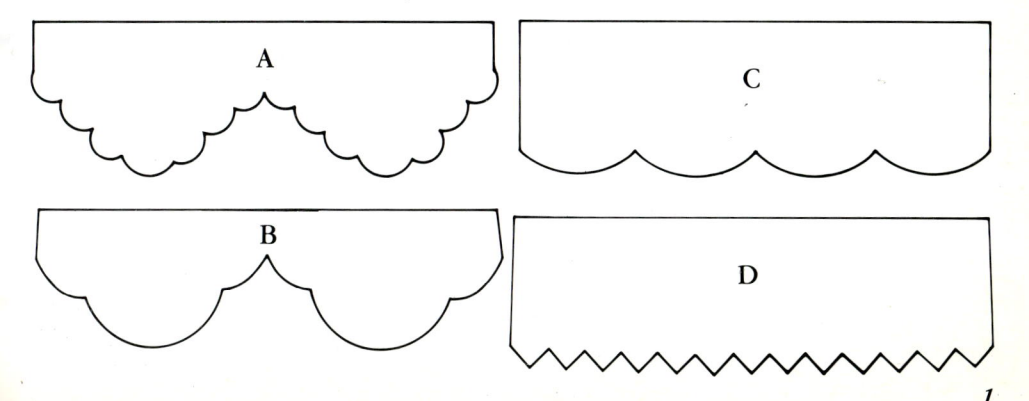

These are made from tin and have good, sharp cutting edges. They need to be washed and dried after use and care should be taken not to bend the top straight edges otherwise the cut pieces of paste will become distorted.

Cutters C, D and the straight Garrett frill cutter can be used in conjunction with cutters A and B if a double frill is required. A frill stamped out from cutters C and D can be cut narrower to give the top half of a double frill.

PREPARATION OF CAKE

A rich fruit cake is undoubtedly the best type of cake to use for this new technique. The cake needs to be at least 2½″ - 3″ (7-8cm) deep, as the decoration emphasis is on the side. A sponge cake of that depth might well sag with the weight of the frill.

The chosen cake can be of any shape — round, square, petal, oval, diamond, fluted oval, heart, trefoil or hexagonal. The cake board should be at least 1½″ (4cm) larger all round than the cake, otherwise the overall finished look will be top-heavy and out of proportion.

Step 1: Cut the cake top level if it has risen during cooking.
Step 2: Thinly spread the apricot jam on the top only.
Step 3: Roll out two thirds of the marzipan until it is about ¼″ (1cm) thick and a good 1″ (2.5cm) larger than the cake. Keep the underside of the marzipan well dusted with icing sugar to prevent it sticking.

Fig. 1

Fig. 2

Fig. 3

Step 4: Put jammed side of cake onto marzipan and cut round exact shape of cake. Pick up cake, marzipan side up, and put to one side.

Step 5: Roll rest of marzipan plus remaining cuttings into a sausage long enough to go round the whole cake. Dust work surface and roll out evenly. The finished strip should be slightly deeper than the cake.

Step 6: Trim off each end and cut straight along one side only. Then roll up like a bandage and stand upright, cut side down.

Step 7: Dust work surface again and reverse cake onto it. Spread jam sparingly round the sides of the cake.

Step 8: Take roll of marzipan and unwind round cake, cutting off surplus when the two ends meet. With a sharp knife trim off surplus marzipan on what will be the bottom of cake. Place right side up in middle of cake board.

You will now have a nice 90° edge to the top of your cake and it is ready for the first coat of royal icing. Ideally the cake should be left for 24 hours for the marzipan to harden off a little. However, if the cake has to be made in a hurry, it can be iced straight away providing the marzipan is not oily (you will know this if your hands became excessively oily whilst rolling out the marzipan).

A royal iced cake should have at least two coats — the first being perfectly dry before putting on the second. When applying the second coat, ice the board after side is completed. To ice a cake successfully it is very necessary to use a turntable, a firm, straight-sided plastic scraper and a solid palette knife. The icing is first spread round the sides with the palette knife, paddling backwards and forwards on each new application in order to get rid of air bubbles. When the complete side is covered, use the scraper to smooth and even out the icing. (The sides only are covered with icing).

Once the sides and board are completely dry, roll out thinly – less than ¼″ (0.5cm) – some sugar paste either slightly larger than the top of the cake or cut out a circle of greaseproof paper with the same diameter as the top of the cake to use as a pattern to cut round. With a pastry brush, very sparingly brush the marzipan on top of the cake with water. With the aid of a rolling pin lift up the sugar paste and lay on top of the cake. Roll pin lightly over, trim off surplus and press down edges with thumb. No marzipan should be showing.

The next stage is to make the thin "tablecloth" throw-over piece onto which you will attach the broderie anglaise.

With the aid of a tape measure, calculate the exact width of the top of the cake, plus 1½″ extra either side. For example, a 10″ (25.5cm) cake will now become 13″ (33cm). Draw on a sheet of greaseproof paper a 13″ (33cm) circle, square, hexagon, etc. and cut out. Roll out some sugar paste to about ⅛″ (0.6cm) thickness, place on your pattern and cut round. Again just dampen top of cake with water, lift the sugar paste with rolling pin and put onto cake leaving the 1½″ surplus falling over sides.

Because the paste is thin it might well stretch; also it is quite possible not to get it perfectly even all round. This is no great problem because the paste can be treated exactly like material and trimmed round evenly with a pair of scissors.

Trim level with scissors

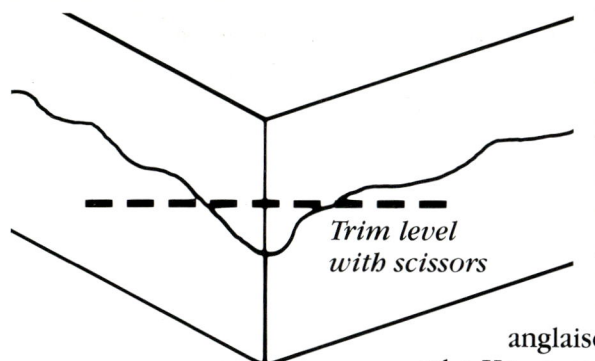

When the surplus paste falls over the edge of the cake it will quite naturally flute out. This adds to the finished effect of the broderie anglaise. Round cakes tend to flute better than square ones — with square and hexagonal cakes the points of the sugar paste have to be trimmed off if you wish the broderie anglaise to be the same depth all round cake. However, points can be left if desired and the finished effect is rather like a handkerchief. The cake must now be left for 24 hours for the paste to harden off. If the frill were added at this stage the flutes would flatten out and the weight of the frill would cause the tablecloth to stretch.

THE BRODERIE ANGLAISE FRILL
(DESIGNED WITH THE BABER CUTTERS)

Each cutter is 5″ (12.5cm) long, making this a quick way to decorate a cake. The frill is attached to the "tablecloth" with royal icing piped on with a no.1 tube. Sticking with egg white is not satisfactory as the frill will slip off.

Roll out the soft icing as thinly as possible and cut out six or seven pieces at a time. Cover pieces with a thin piece of plastic (plastic shopping bags cut to size will do very well) to stop them drying. Using one cut piece at a time stamp out the traditional broderie anglaise pattern. Cocktail sticks will make round holes, matchsticks - square ones. The tiny pear-shaped aspic cutter will make a five or three petal shape or even a spring type blossom cutter can be used. A quarter-inch metal piping tube, pinched on one side, will also make a peardrop shape.

Just up from the bottom edge of the tablecloth pipe a line of icing the length of your frill and attach frill by pressing onto icing with left hand and playing out the frill with right hand until the whole length is stuck firmly (see fig. 5).

When attaching the next piece of frill keep it as near to its predecessor as possible, leaving no gaps. Carry on right round the cake. If luck is on your side (and it seldom is) the pieces will all fit in nicely. However, nothing is ever straightforward and you will probably find that you have a final gap smaller than the size of the

Fig. 4

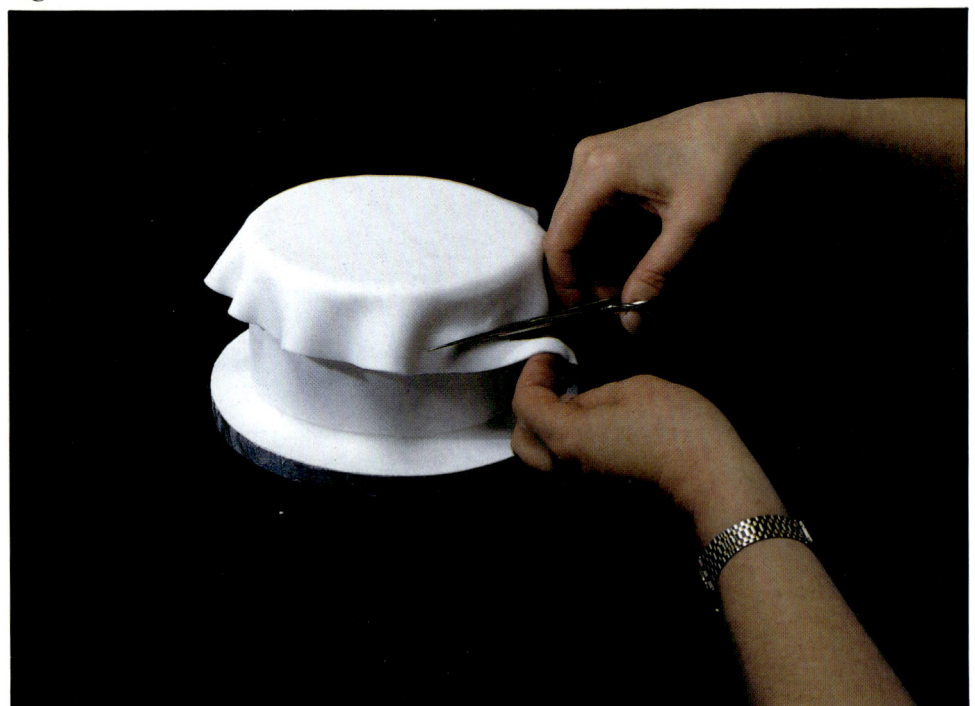

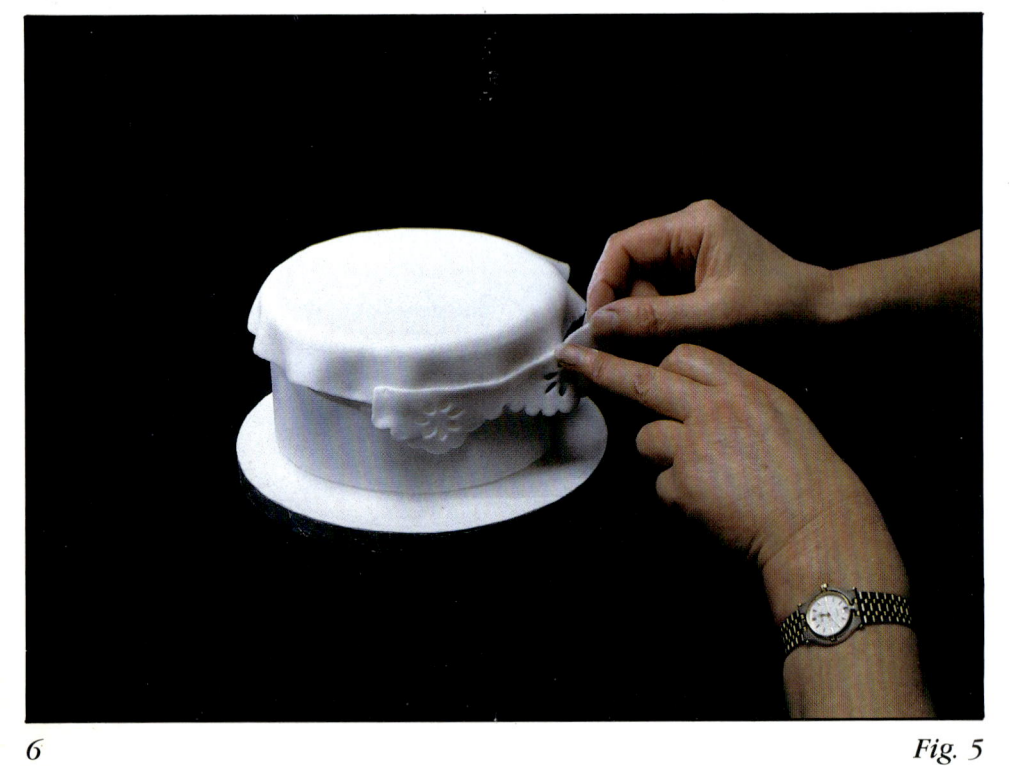

6

Fig. 5

cut piece. With cutters C and D there is not really a problem — you just cut them to size by measuring the gap and fitting the odd piece in, putting that section to the back of your cake. Cutters A and B, however, take a little more working out. For example:

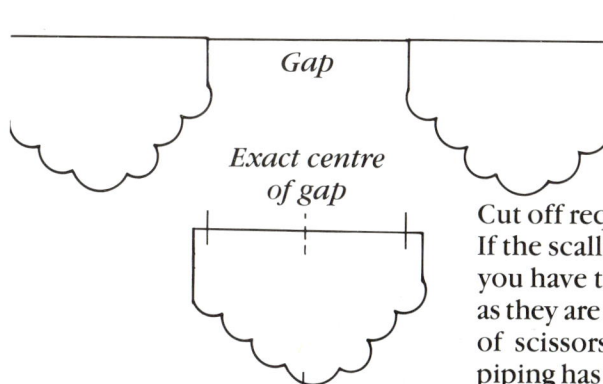

Take the measurement of the gap and put it against one scallop of the frill, with the exact centre of the measurement in the exact centre of the frill.

Cut off required size and fit this into gap. If the scallops do not exactly match then you have two choices: either leave them as they are or trim off carefully with a pair of scissors. Either way, once the over-piping has been done, the odd frill will be difficult to detect.

Double Frill

This is about ¼ of the depth of the under-frill and is cut out with either C or D cutters or a straight Garrett frill cutter. It is attached with icing sugar slightly above the original frill, not right on the edge because this makes the top edge

Fig. 6

rather thick. Once again, all holes are punched in on the table top and are usually just a single line of small holes or squares. When attaching this top frill follow the line of the original frill. This will keep all the joins in the same places.

When all the broderie anglaise is in place it is then overpiped with a "0" piping tube. All holes are piped round, as are the bottom edges of scallops, dots, leaves, stems, small daisies and tiny curved lines, which can be piped onto the frill, as, in fact, can any design that can be found on a piece of broderie anglaise. Inspiration can be sought from bed linen, towels, blouses, collars, underwear, petticoats — anything trimmed with broderie anglaise.

To finish the top edge, pipe neat and very small dots between the join of the frill and the tablecloth. No broderie anglaise would be complete without ribbon, either as an insertion or very thin flat ribbons stuck on singly or in a double line, frequently enhanced with a small bow.

RIBBON INSERTION *(see fig. 6)*

This is usually done, in the case of a cake, just above the frill. Trying to do it on the frill itself would be extremely hazardous as it has no solid backing. The holes would stretch and the frill could well fall off. If you are very clever it could be inserted whilst the frill is still flat on the table, with a length of ribbon, but again the holes tend to stretch whilst pulling the ribbon through. The safest method is the one shown in the photographs.

Fig. 7

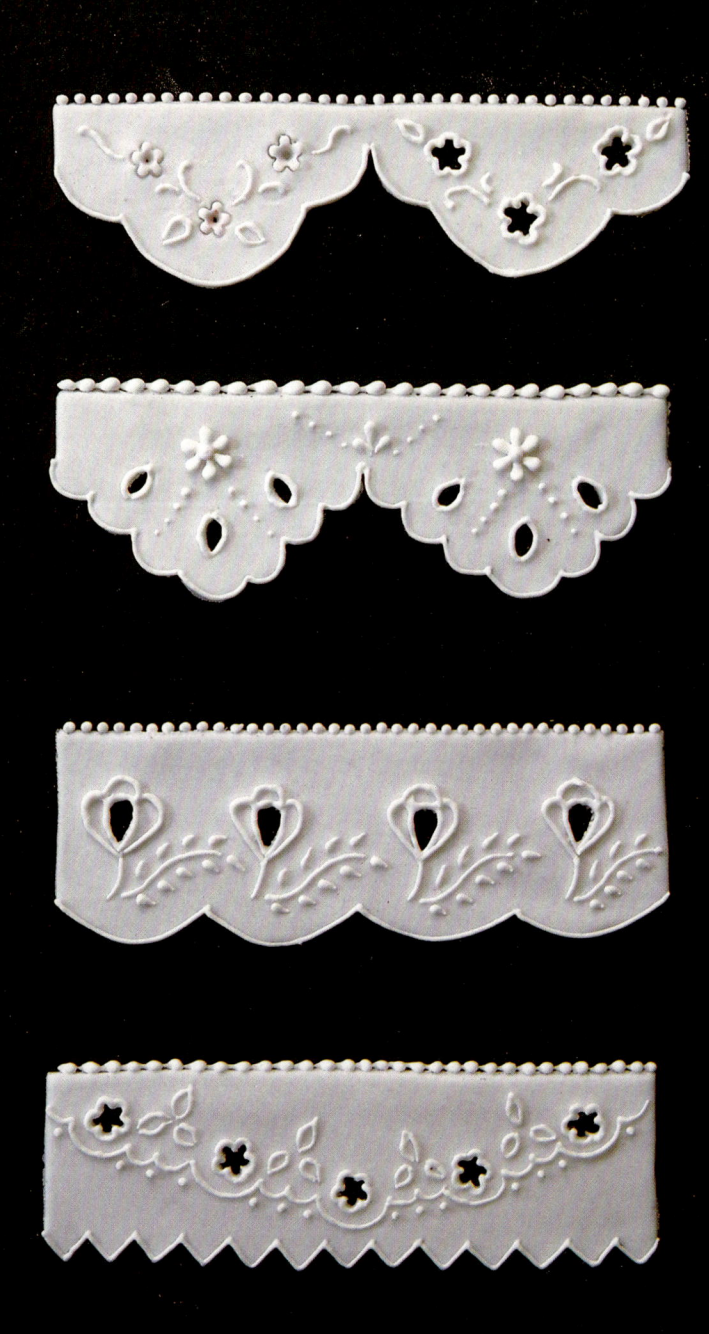

Method

With the ribbon-threading tool, cut two vertical lines approximately ¼" (0.5cm) apart then cut two more approximately ½" (1.5cm) apart and so on, all round the cake.

| | | | | | | | | | | |

Tear off a piece of ribbon the same thickness as the cut. Slot one end into each left-hand slit, then, with the left forefinger holding the ribbon steady, take the ribbon tool in the right hand and bend ribbon over towards the right slot and poke in. Gaps between the ribbon can be decorated with tiny dots or left plain.

Note: A whole piece of ribbon can be threaded into the top piece of a double frill, see fig. 9. It is done whilst the sugar paste is still pliable and before attaching to cake.

VARIATIONS ON A THEME

1. Coat the sides of the cake with icing in a deeper shade than that of the broderie anglaise. This will make the frill stand out more sharply.
2. Attach a fairly deep band of ribbon to the cake around the upper middle, making sure the bottom of the frill is lower than the ribbon. The colour of the ribbon will show through the cut-out holes.
3. Throw a square or hexagonal "tablecloth" over a round cake and attach a piece of broderie anglaise frill half the size of the cutter round the edge. This would be best done with cutters C and D as the frill is too deep on cutters A and B.
4. Attach little clusters of blossoms at intervals to the top edge of the frill where it joins the "tablecloth", either in a colour to match the ribbon or with the centres of the flowers piped in the same colour as the ribbon.
5. Attach pieces of piped lace round the bottom edge of the frill. Frills from B and C cutters have the best edges for added lacework.
6. Pipe tiny dots in groups of three, in a delicate contrasting colour to the main cake, all over the iced side. This not only gives a texture to the surface of the icing – it also has the appearance of very fine dotted muslin.
7. With a very small tube ("0" or "00") pipe fine cornelli on sides of cake before putting on the frill.
8. Pipe a piquet edging round frills (cut with B or C cutters). This is done with a fine tube ("0" or "00") - you just pipe three small dots close together but not touching, leave a small space of about ¼" then pipe three more, same space apart and so on, until you arrive back where you started. Then pipe two small dots in between the three and eventually finish with one dot. The final effect is that of little points of lace edging the frill.

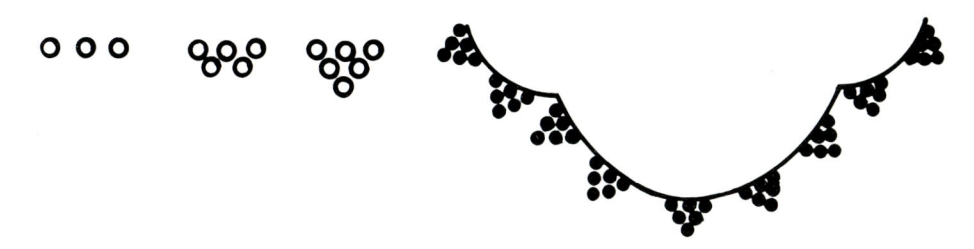

9. Pipe loops round the edge of frill. Pipe crossed loops round edge of frill.

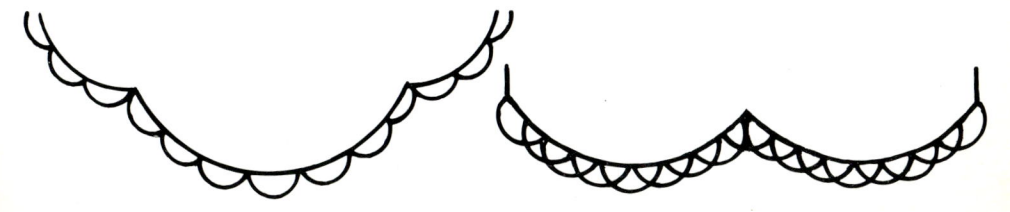

Fig. 8

Fig. 9

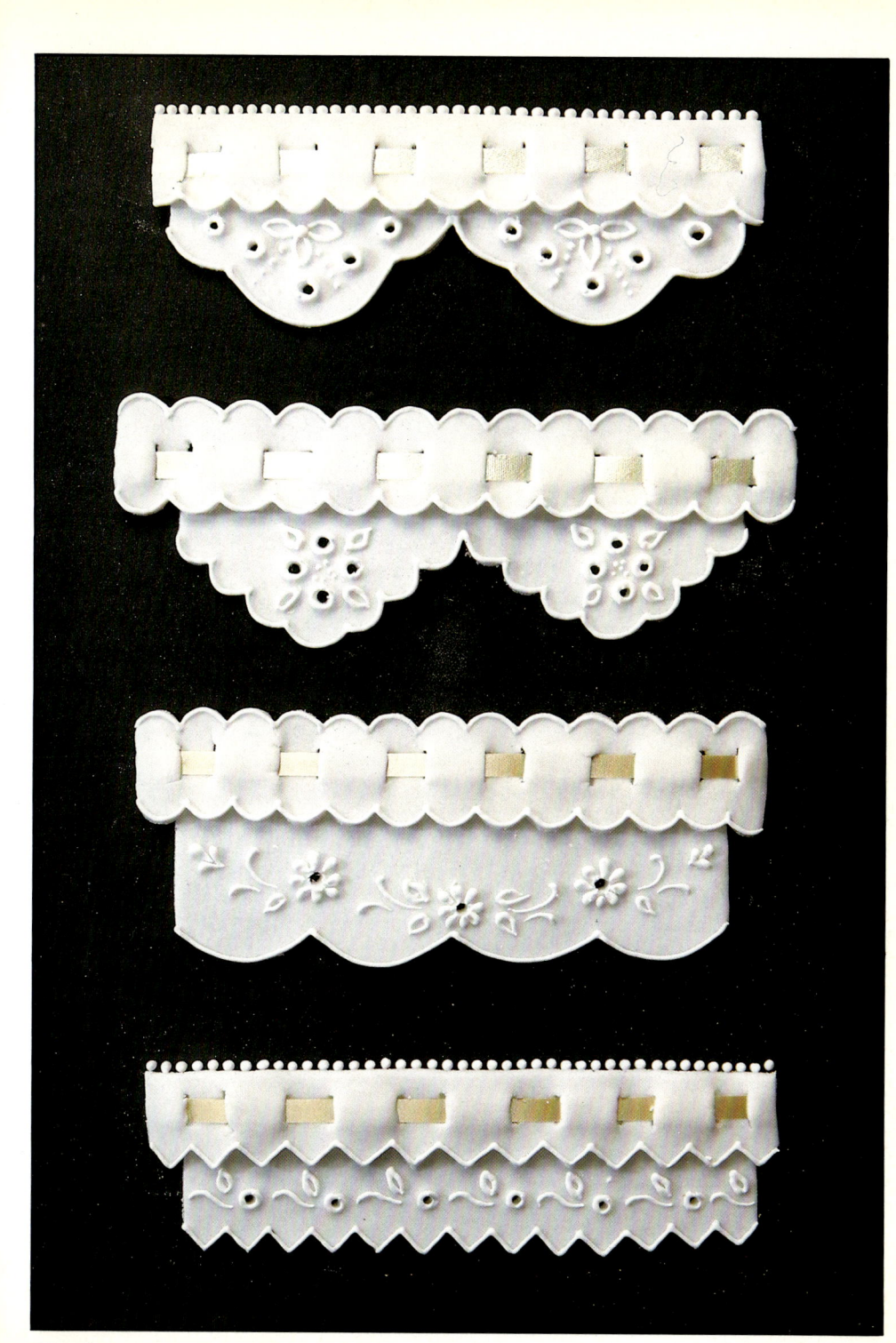

10. Instead of piping a straight line round the edge of the frill, try:

(a) tiny dots

(b) a very small shell border

(c) a very thin rope

11. Using frill from cutters B or C, frill the edges with a cocktail stick using the same technique you would for a Garrett frill. The finished effect is not broderie anglaise but is, nevertheless, very pretty. It can still be cut out and "embroidered" as with the other frills, the edges also can be lightly tinted with edible coloured dust to match ribbons or flowers, giving an enchanting overall appearance.
12. Using a straight Garrett frill, cut out a piece of sugar paste. Turn cutter round and cut scallops on the straight side ½" down from the straight top edge.

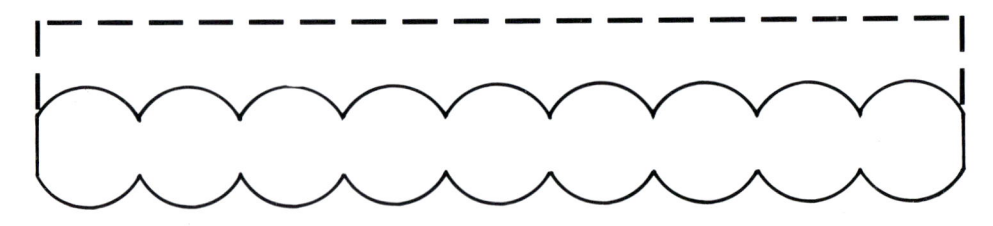

14

13. Attach to side of cake with royal icing. In the middle, top edge or bottom edge with the ribbon insertion tool cut slits and insert ribbon, finishing with a little bow.

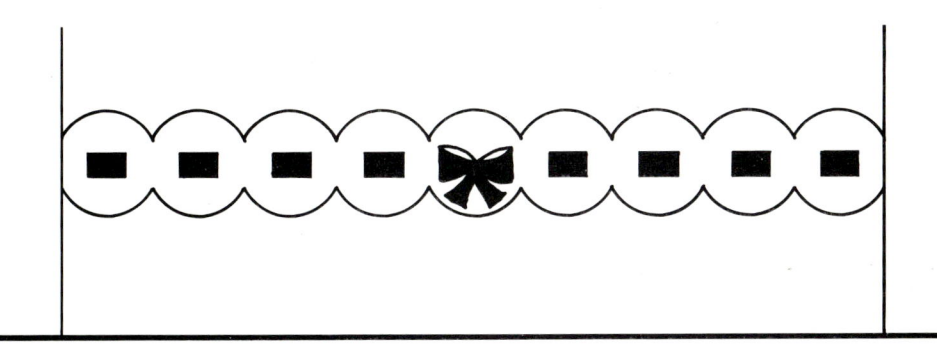

This is particularly suitable for Christening Cakes or cakes that are not too deep. It can also be used in conjunction with bridge extension work or with a straight garrett frill.

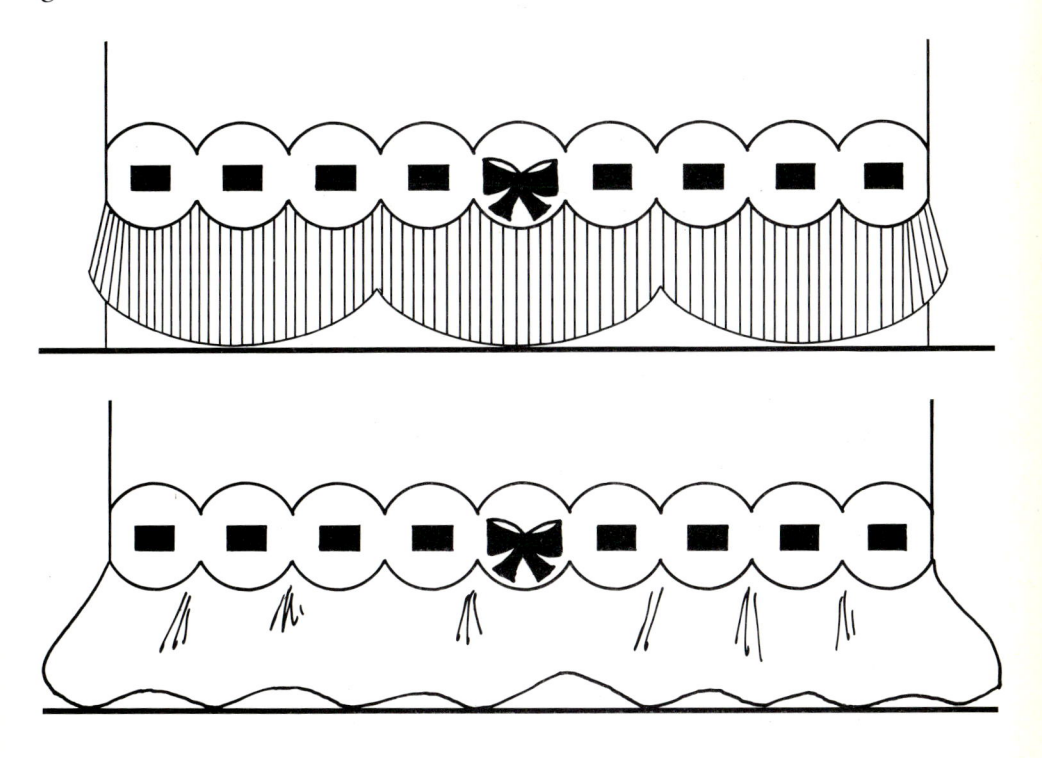

Note: With bridge extension work make sure you attach the broderie anglaise frill before piping the lines. One slip of the frill will break the fine piping.

Fig. 10

Fig. 11

16

OTHER IDEAS

Handkerchief

An attractive idea for the top of a young girl's birthday cake or a cake for a lady.
    Roll out some white or coloured sugar paste and cut into a square. The size will depend on the amount of space available on the top of the cake. Roll out some more paste and cut out the frills, preferably with cutters C or D or a straight Garrett frill. Cut off one third from straight edge. The frills should be longer than each side of the square in order to mitre the corners. This will probably mean a join in the frills — if this is the case make sure the join comes in the middle of the square.

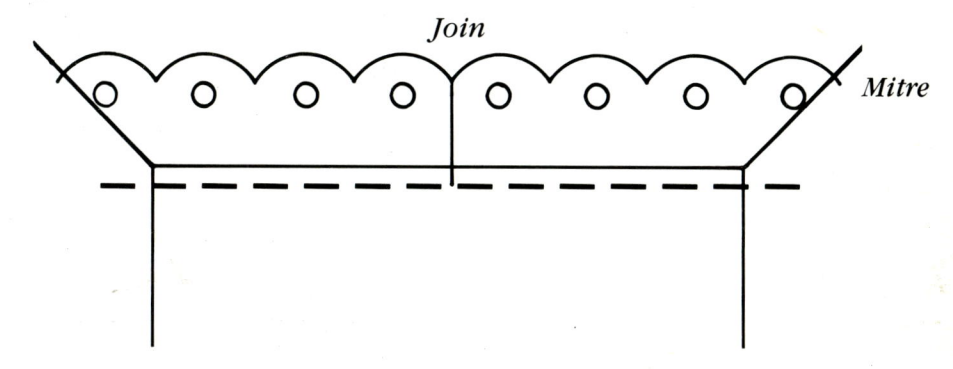

Mark holes before attaching to square. When frills have been firmly fixed, with the aid of a palette knife fold one corner to the opposite one and then in half again. Complete handkerchief by overpiping holes and outside edge of frill.

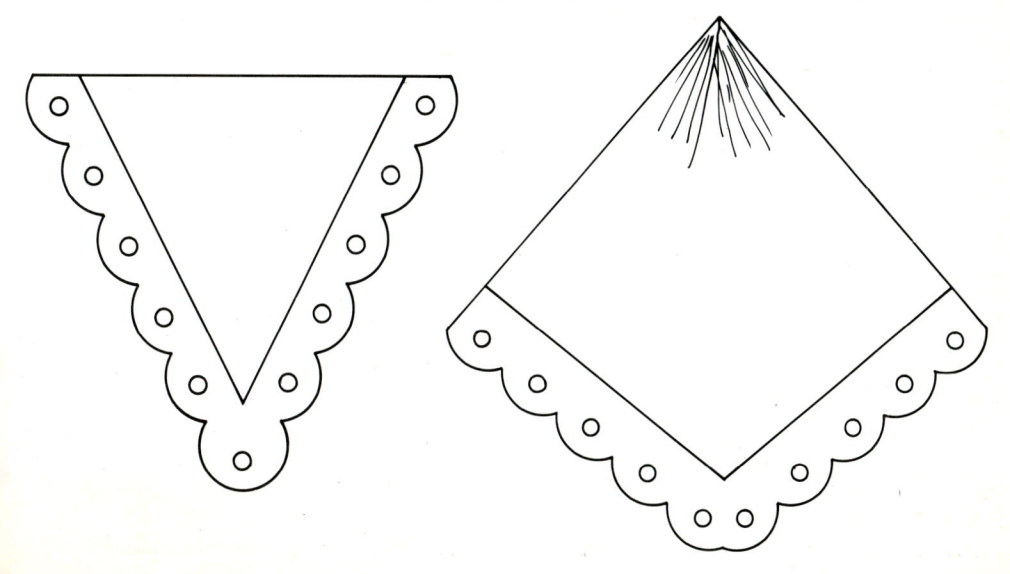

Initials can then be piped onto the corner of the handkerchief and maybe a single rose laid either by the side of it or on it.

Note: A couple of pencils laid under the top layer of the handkerchief and left overnight will give folds to the "material" and therefore produce a more realistic effect.

A very thin straight ribbon attached just above the join of the frill to handkerchief is much easier than trying to insert ribbon. Finish with tiny dots where handkerchief joins frill.

Note: To gauge size of handkerchief cut out some squares of greaseproof paper in different sizes, fold over and try each one on top of the cake in order to determine which one looks best.

Serviette

Marvellous party pieces for a very special occasion.

Make some swiss rolls approximately one quarter of the thickness of the average roll and about 6" (15cm) long. Roll out some marzipan very thinly and cover rolls, cutting out two round pieces to cover each end. Attach marzipan to rolls with a very thin layer of butter cream rather than jam.

Roll out sugar paste very thinly and cut out two circles to cover each end of roll. Attach with either a dab of water or a little icing sugar. Roll out more sugar paste and cut slightly wider than the roll and long enough to wrap round the roll one and a half times. Cut a wide "V" on the edge of the paste and wrap round the roll, with the V edge facing upwards.

Cut out broderie anglaise frill, mark holes and attach to edge of V with royal icing. Overpipe, insert ribbon, pipe dots at join and pipe the initial of guest onto serviette.

Christmas Cracker

Again using a small swiss roll, proceed as for serviette by covering with marzipan and attaching circles of sugar paste to each end of roll. Take some more sugar paste and roll out thinly. Cut just enough to wrap around the roll and measure exact width of roll. Wrap round roll and attach with a little water, making sure the join is on the bottom of the roll. Cut out two frills with cutter D. Wrap around end of rolls and trim off surplus. Attach to roll with icing sugar ½" in from each end. Holding join with one hand, lightly pinch extended frill with the other to form cracker ends. In the open space of cracker push a little ball of crumpled tissue paper and leave for 24 hours. Gently remove and overpipe broderie anglaise. Attach a thin red or gold ribbon near the join of frill and pipe dots. A bunch of holly can then be piped onto the cracker or a Christmas rose or poinsettia added.

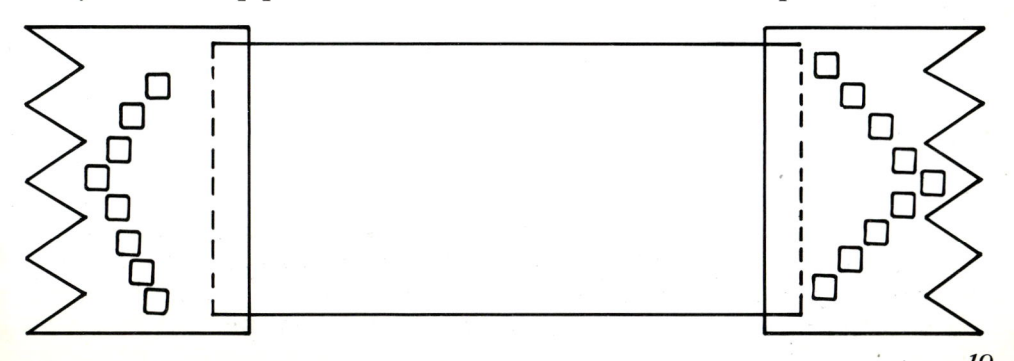

19

Fig. 12

The finishing touch would be a name piped on perhaps in red.

Crinoline Lady

A charming cake for ladies of all ages. The colours chosen for the sugar paste gown can range from pastel to deep scarlet, jade or royal blue, with an underskirt of white, contrasting or toning shades.

To make the cake, use a rich fruit cake recipe and bake in a tin shaped like a pudding basin. When cold, shape the skirt by slicing about one third of the cake off. This will be the front of the dress. The cut piece is then shaped where necessary and attached to the back of the skirt with the aid of boiled apricot jam to give a slight train effect.

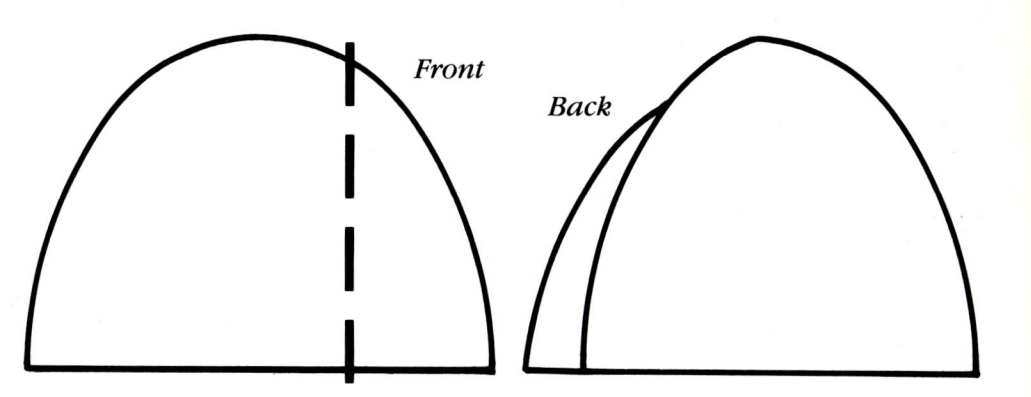

Front

Back

Roll out some marzipan very thinly and cut out a circle. This should be large enough to cover the cake, falling in drapes at the sides and back, straight in the front. Trim off surplus at base of skirt. The cake must be brushed with apricot jam before throwing over the marzipan.

Next, roll out some sugar paste, coloured if required, for the underskirt. Very lightly dampen the marzipan with water before putting on the sugar paste. The sugar paste will fall neatly over the marzipan folds. Trim off surplus but make sure you do not have any marzipan showing.

Ideas for the front of the skirt:

1. A double or treble Garrett frill can be attached with the aid of icing or egg white, each frill shorter in width as you go up towards the waist.
2. Small flowers can be piped onto the sugar paste, coloured dots in groups of three, cornelli piped in a contrasting colour or the colour of the overskirt. Tiny piped flowers look very attractive, or larger flowers using the brush embroidery technique will make the finished gown look very rich.

For the overskirt roll out the coloured sugar paste and cut out a wedge piece one third of the size. With a pair of scissors round off edges. Dampen waist area of underskirt, lift overskirt by slipping hands flat each side of the cut wedge of the sugar paste. Make sure the open piece of overskirt reveals the decoration/frills on front of dress.

The back of the skirt can be lifted in the centre an inch or so at this stage between finger and thumb and secured with a cocktail stick if required, to give added interest. The cocktail stick can be removed after 24 hours and the bunched-up tuck will remain in place.

Lastly, add the broderie anglaise frill by cutting the sugar paste with the straight Garrett frill or C or D cutter. Trim to a depth of about ½". Make the holes in the frill with either a cocktail stick or the end of a small paintbrush. Attach to the gown with royal icing and either insert very narrow ribbon or stick on a single thread of ribbon.

The actual bust of the lady can be purchased at most sugar craft shops and is the final addition to the cake. Attach with a little royal icing to the skirt. Tie a sash of ribbon around the waist to conceal the join. For presentation cover a cake board with some dark coloured material and set the crinoline lady slightly back from the centre. Cut out a small oval plaque from white sugar paste or make a run-out plaque and pipe on the recipient's name.

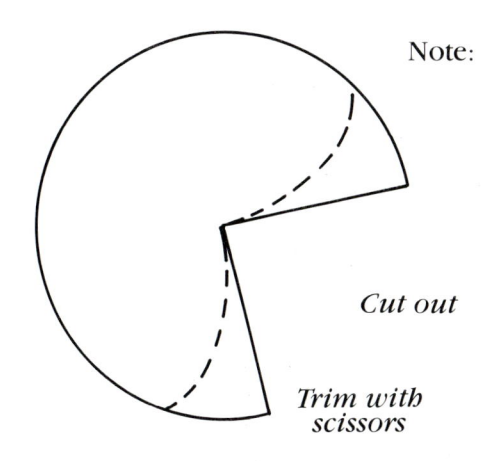

Note: If necessary, trim off a little cake at the top to keep the waist area small. Put the cake on a very small straw board the same size as the base of the cake, cutting off front to match. This makes it much easier to lift off the work surface onto cake board when the skirt is completed.

Buy the bust for the crinoline lady first and set it on top of your cake tin in order to judge the finished perspective.

Cut out

Trim with scissors

CUSHION

Bake a 10" – 12" (25.5 – 30.5cm) square rich fruit cake about 2" (5cm) in depth. When cold, trim edges to give an outward slope on all four sides.

Cake

Fig. 13

With a sharp knife cut a wide inward curve on each side of cake.

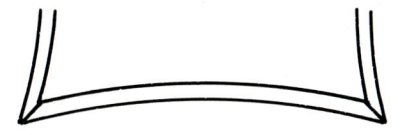

Spread sieved apricot jam very thinly all over the cake. Measure the cake from side to side, taking tape measure to bottom edges of cake each side. Place cake on a board 1″ – 1½″ (2.5 – 4cm) larger than the cake. Roll out some marzipan to approximately ¼″ (0.5cm) thick and a good 1″ (2.5cm) larger than the measurements.

Pick up marzipan with a rolling pin and put onto cake. Smooth marzipan over cake starting from the centre with flat hands and work outwards. Trim off surplus at edges of cake. The sugar paste is rolled out in the same manner as the marzipan, i.e. by measuring cake. Before rolling on, remember to brush a little water very sparingly over the marzipan. Smooth down, trim off edges.

Make a rope of sugar paste for edge of cushion by rolling very thin lengths of sugar paste (perhaps two different colours) and twist together. Attach to base of cushion with egg white.

Cut frill from A, B, C or D cutters, stamp out holes and attach in a square onto cake. The frill should hang down slightly over edges but not right to the board, obscuring the rope. Overpipe cut outs and pipe tiny dots where frill joins sugar paste. Then either insert ribbon or attach a length of ribbon just above frill. Finally, pipe inscription on top of cake and add a spray of flowers.

These cushions look delightful in white or shades of cream, pink and lavender.

RECIPES

Note: g = gram, Kg = kilogram, ml = millilitre, dl = decilitre, l = litre.
1Kg = 1,000g (2lb), 500g = 1lb, 100ml = 1dl, 10dl = 1 litre.

Rich Fruit Cake

12oz (360g) white fat (not lard)
12oz (360g) margarine
1½ lb (800ml) dark brown sugar
(muscavados or bababos)
1½ pints (800ml) egg
2lb (1Kg) strong white flour
(bread flour)
7lb (3.5Kg) mixed dried fruit
(currants, raisins, sultanas)

1lb (0.5Kg) ground almonds
1lb (0.5Kg) glacé cherries washed
and dried
Grated zest and juice of two
lemons and two oranges
Mixed spice
Caramel colouring

Made by the sugar batter method.

1. Cream fats and sugar together at a high speed until quite pale in colour, scrape down bowl.
2. Add eggs gradually, still beating fast. Stop machine and scrape down bowl frequently.
3. Turn machine on to low speed and add flour and ground almonds.
4. Add mixed spice and caramel colour. Colour must be judged, remembering that the cake will darken with cooking.
5. On slow speed pour in fruit juices and zest.
6. Add mixed fruit (still on slow speed).
7. Lastly, put in cherries, mixing slowly and taking care not to break them up.

This quantity of cake mix equals 16½ lb (8.25Kg) and is sufficient for a three-tier wedding cake divided in the following manner:

10" tin 7/8lb (3.5/4Kg)
8" tin 4lb (2Kg)
6" tin 2lb (1Kg)

12" tin 9½ lb (4.5Kg)
9" tin 5lb (2.5Kg)
6" tin 2lb (1Kg)

Cake tin should be lightly greased and lined with greaseproof paper. Wrap round the tins about ten sheets of newspaper tied with string. Place the tins on a sheet of cardboard in the oven and put another piece of cardboard over the cake tin. This will allow the cake to cook through without burning the sides; the sheet of cardboard on the top of the cake tin helps to keep the surface flat. Bake at gas mark 3 (300°F or 150°C).

Note: Alcohol is best added to cakes after baking as it evaporates during

Fig. 14

cooking. Turn cakes over and spike bottom with a sharp knife and pour in either brandy, sweet sherry or rum. Too much alcohol will make the cake soggy and can also cause the marzipan to become sticky.

Sugar Paste

2lb (1Kg) icing sugar
½ oz (15g) white vegetable fat
1 heaped teaspoon powder gelatine

1 egg white
8oz (250g) liquid glucose
2 tablespoons cold water

1. Put cold water in small cup, sprinkle on gelatine and leave for a few minutes, then stand in hot water until mixture is perfectly clear.
2. Stand jar of glucose in very hot water until if softens, dip a tablespoon into boiling water and spoon out glucose. Four good tablespoons equal approximately 8oz (250g).
3. Sieve icing sugar straight onto a clean work surface and make a largish well in the middle.
4. Into the well pour gelatine, egg white and liquid glucose. Mix thoroughly with tips of fingers then gradually draw in icing sugar.
5. Knead all ingredients together. When a soft ball has formed knead in the white fat. If the mixture is too dry, add more egg white; if too soft, more icing sugar.

Note: Many supermarkets and most sugar craft shops sell a good ready-made sugar paste.

Royal Icing

1 fresh egg white (grade 2 egg = 1oz (30g)
(3oz (90g) powdered egg white is reconstituted with
1 pint (0.5 litre) cold water – 20oz = 1 pint)
7lb (3.5Kg) icing sugar to 1 pint (0.5 litre) egg white
7oz (210g) icing sugar to 1¼ oz (31ml) egg white

Lemon juice or acetic acid will harden royal icing, glycerine will soften.
A few drops of blue colouring added during beating produces snow-white royal icing.

1. Put sieved icing sugar into a machine bowl and pour on egg white. Use the beater attachment.
2. Beat on speed 3/4 until the icing will stand in a peak. To test, dip a palette knife into the mixture, draw out and hold upright. If sugar on the end of

the knife stands up without curling it is ready for use.
3. If beating by hand use a wooden spoon, hold bowl at an angle with one hand and beat steadily with the other until required consistency is reached.

South African Modelling Paste

2 cups sieved icing sugar
1 rounded teaspoon gelatine
1 large egg white (remove string)
1 tablespoon water
3 teaspoons gum tragacanth
1 teaspoon vegetable fat (Trex)

1. Grease bowl with white fat and place over hot water. Add gum tragacanth and one cup of icing (sieved). Warm to 98°F.
2. Place water and gelatine together and dissolve.
3. Beat egg white slightly and add to icing together with the gelatine. Beat until creamy. Cool.
4. Work in balance of icing sugar. Grease hands and knead well. Store in a plastic bag.

Note: 1. Cup sizes vary — if finished paste is too soft add a little more icing; if too stiff a little more egg white.
2. Put water and gelatine in a small cup and stand in hot water until quite clear.

HANDY HINTS

(a) When colouring sugar paste, pinch off a small piece of paste and colour darker than required shade. Gradually add white paste to it until you reach the colour of your choice.

(b) For royal icing mix a few drops of water into powder colours before mixing — this will prevent any speckling.

(c) Invest in a compass for drawing circular patterns. Always draw patterns on white or greaseproof paper, as newsprint has been known to mark sugar paste and royal icing.

(d) When cutting round patterns from sugar paste use a sharp pointed knife, hold upright to table and cut a continuous line wherever possible.

(e) Rule of thumb for quantity of marzipan required for a cake is to use half the weight of the cake, e.g. 10lb (5Kg) cake — 5lb (2.5Kg) marzipan.

(f) Always keep royal icing covered with a damp cloth.

(g) The same batch of icing can be used for up to a week, re-beaten successfully each day.

(h) Rich fruit cakes can be put into tins and refrigerated for several days should you not wish to cook them all at once. Once out of the refrigerator let them stand to reach room temperature before baking.

(i) Raw cake mix can be deep frozen in plastic containers should you have some left over.

(j) Baked cakes should be wrapped in non-porous covering, e.g. tin foil, to stop drying and bacterial spoilage.

(k) Left-over iced cakes, e.g. top tier of wedding cake, can be stored in the same manner, but remove from cake board first.

(l) If your cake batter starts to curdle — don't worry, add either the ground almonds or half a pound of flour with the last addition of egg, beat well and the curdle will come out.

Fig. 15

+++ **STOP PRESS** +++

The following cutters, which can be used in conjunction with the Baber frill to produce broderie anglaise, are now available.

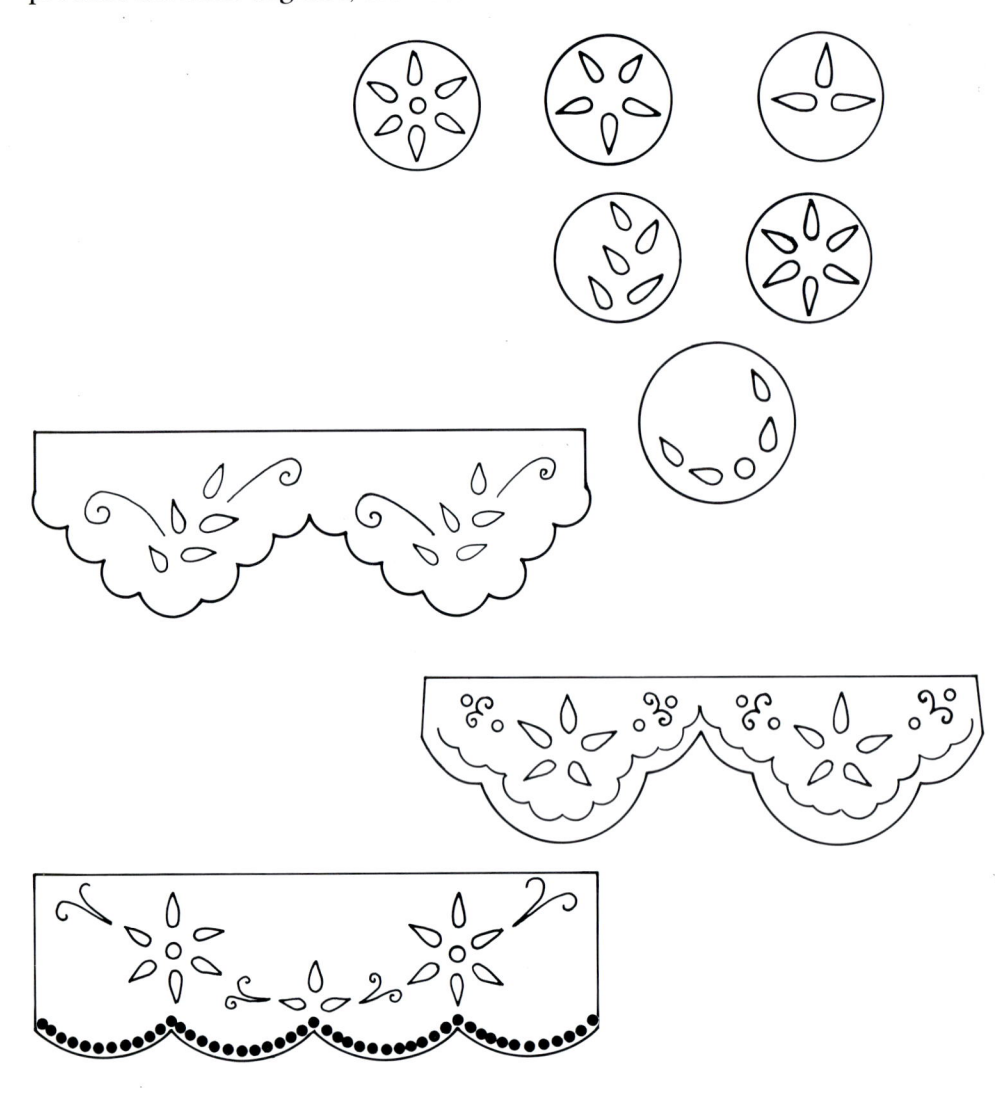